Meeting Dusk

Niobe Melendy

BookLeaf Publishing

India | USA | UK

Presentation by *BookLeaf Publishing*

Web: www.bookleafpub.com

E-mail: info@bookleafpub.com

ISBN: 9789357445764

First edition 2022

DEDICATION

For Nikos. The world really isn't so big after all.

How To

The second result on Google for 'how to' is
How to write poetry
Like it isn't something that simply springs
Fully formed from the Earth
Every nocturne tilled from the night
Every sonata harvested from the where the
waves crash
A sound woven into silence
Held in the gentle hands of words
That know only peace
Like these words are chosen by us
Like the world hasn't handed them freely over
And like we have any choice in it

There is only one step to writing poetry
It is to feel a series of emotions
That words half capture in some facsimile
Of being

Death

You that grew
And you that loved and lied and died
I see you now
And you can rest now

You, like your forefathers,
You saw the world and it was wonderful
And you loved your children as your father
loved you
And you do not fade
Now that you are home
You can rest now

You that grew
And you that came home to me
You that ran from me and hid from me
Like I was here to hurt you
You can stop running now
And you that avoided thinking of me
Because I was the greatest unknown you ever
knew

You can know me now

Your life was long and lovely
And you did all that you could
And you did it so well
And your touch lives on in the world you don't
And I am so proud of you
And you can rest now

Older in an Airport

I am standing in an airport
And my mom is dropping me off
I stand in line at airport security
She says goodbye because this is where we part
And this is my second year leaving for school
I did not cry like this last time

She walks away and I am crying
And some kind stranger turns to me
His son went to college and did this too
I cried for the rest of the month
When I was alone

These changes are good
They lead me on
And I am learning and stumbling
Growing
My childhood is old
It wanes as it should
But I am change resistant
And I don't know if I can find the ring I lost
If there is no one to ask for help
And how do I go to the post office and talk to
The stranger behind the desk

If my dad doesn't take me there and ask for me

I am back in the airport
Waiting in line and my mom is talking to me
I try to convince myself this is fine
I want to risk and learn and change
I want to grow
I don't want to lose this

Starry Night

This night is too beautiful to know alone
The stars fall across the sky as silk
I am younger walking alone
Asking my friends not to jaywalk
Because I was nearly hit by a car
And we laugh and I'm sad
But we laugh anyways because I'm always sad
And I will be better when high school is over
And college is over
And when I am abroad maybe I am happy
someday
But tonight is too beautiful to know alone
And I am not happy
But the moon is and the stars are
And the breeze is singing on the water
Sailing under the gate and going out to sea
So here I am
Sad
Sharing it with you
Because there is too much joy here to be lost
And this night is too beautiful to be known alone

A Quiet Breath of Air

There is a breath of air
Held still and quiet
Held between the water
That distorts the light
And the sky
That is endless and ends here
I do not exist

There is a breath of air that does not move
Though the tide does and the sky does
And the satellites crawl slow across
The greatest wild we will never know
The breath of air is still and cool
I do not exist

The breath of air moves when the light crosses
From the edge of the sea to where I sleep here
And wake to some new age

The world begins to turn again
And all of this exists
But the breath of air is gone

All The Same

Cycles of change
Are but cycles of the same
Under a different name

If change is the only constant
Then constantly changing is all the same
And I have been here before
And so have the ones that came before me
They were here in this moment
All that time ago
When they stepped up to this same precipice
I stand upon now
And they called it new
And they called it exciting
Because that's what it is
I am the new cycle
But I have been here before too
So the cycle is shorter than me
Which is rather unusual for something to be

And the cycle begins anew
It does not wait if I am ready
It does not wait for anybody

This change is fine

I guess

The Writing

The writing happens at 2 am
When I can't sleep and the coyotes
Bark and howl behind the dark
And on those car rides
Typing on my phone
Getting carsick to remember
These fleeting feelings before they
Disappear forever
And it happens next to conversations
I am not a part of
And in the shower
Where the paper falls apart
So I have to say these words
Over and over
Remember
And hope they don't escape me
Before the water dries

Burn

It was once beautiful when the sky
Turned red-orange at end of day
A beauty to be chased and admired
Until it went away
Because it went away
In a moment

Now the sky is orange because it burns
And, yes, there is a beauty to it
But the sun glares unendingly red
And so many questions go unsaid
It asks us why we did this
It demands we count our dead
And are we happy yet?

When the world ended
The skies burned
And I thought we would have learned

For Language

In words, in language, in a voice not known
To a tune lilting in the afternoon
In a garden these words have overgrown
These travelling words, they approach so soon
Carried by a music this language sings
Sang to a melody foreign to me
This new language carried this music brings
Lightly and gently, as though it were free
Every word, every sound, how they call
I would like to think like I could learn them all

A Word Like Serenade

This planet is a most prolific writer
Who created words like amor and serenade
And I speak none
And know less
I do not listen
I am too young to learn
There is too much to see
And too little time
I can learn when I have grown old
And the world does not know my name
For she does now
And she does not try to teach now
She knows I will not listen
And there is all the time in the world
When I am dead
To learn a word like serenade

Roots

The light fades slow
The sun is near rest
And it misses me
I am home
I am paying no attention
I do not ask where it is going
I just know that the light at my window
Is somewhere between my blinds
And the neighbor's house
And maybe hiding somewhere
I care too little to look for
I'm reading a book
It smells like childhood and adventure
Like home
And the pages are delicate
And my tea is hot
And I am unaware that the light is fading
Until the sun is gone and the world turns dark
And I cannot read anymore

Branches

The water is ink
The sky is dark
There are roots of light in the sky
Whose branches touch the ocean
And this is the same ocean from home
My roots
And it is so far that I have come
My branches
And there is a place far off
That they meld into one concept
Sky and here
Ocean and home
It is too dark to see the difference
The sky is ink
The water is dark
I am here now

Passage

We unbecome the past into the future.
Some new discovery propels us forwards
And up into stars
And below seas
And to where we are already.
Time is chaos incarnate.
We know tangible chaos is
Who we will be tomorrow
And what we make of it
And nothing more.

I boil water and blow a fuse
And all of my outlets are dead
So the flowers wither to be replaced
And the breaker box is somewhere here
But powerless is how we always are -
Powerless to the steady pace of time
And the chaos in its wake.
There is no point in finding the breaker box.
The outlets are dead in this and every moment,

So are the flowers,
So am I.
I was born to live and die
And time will not love me enough
To rest for even a moment.
I will not be remembered in any other way
Than in a cup of black coffee,
In the torture of a young violin,
Or in the words I used to say
Like it will be what it will be
Like I want to know all there is to see,
And I'm okay with that.
Time will love me enough
To say my name like this.

I am powerless enough to be powerless.
I unbecome myself into who I will be tomorrow
And I will unbecome myself into nothing
But the waves and the tide
And I will be forgotten
By the people who did not know me
When I drove past them or
Bumped into them briefly.
Time will not tell them my name.
Time will let me rest.

I Exist

I exist tonight and yesterday
I may tomorrow in some way
If I'm unlucky
Or unlucky

I simply am

Tonight my window is open
And the gentle whispers of the tide
Drift in on the breeze
The voice of the train blows brazenly by
And there are so many people behind the trees
Living lives I will never know

I will live until I die
Life will blow gently by
The rise the fall the in between
I will live to learn and live to see
I will die when my light is lost
I exist and I will not

Foresight

I moved away for school in a torrent
Of confusion and carsick conversations
I cried and we hugged and I was alone

My parents went home
Then my brother went home
And then it was just me

My new room is full of just my things
My hands are empty
My future is tenuous
My past is tired
My childhood is grown
Sitting on the doorstep watching my brother
drive away
I knew these tears were going to happen for
days

The tears come anyways

My family disperses
Across a thousand little miles
Beyond state lines of time change

And the walls of various snow caps and corn
fields
That bear no meaningful names
My childhood is over
But it was over years ago
My childhood bedroom was redecorated
Long ago the sheets were changed
Yesterday
When I first left
It was time to move on

The tears come anyways

Stars At Rest

As the tide disappears it is early.
The rest of my neighborhood is asleep
Wrapped in the sheets of the dark,
But I am not and neither is she -
She, the little fairy, and me.
She flits around the water softly,
Keeping her little toes damp and salty.
Her light flickers each moment to the other,
Like the hands of the tired tide hold her.
I am astounded that she is here -
But then she descends and disappears
Into the folds of glittering tide
Where the rest of the stars are asleep.

A Man About A Dog (I Want to Go Home)

The night is young - her freckles shine,
But something in my mind grows old.
Some tired puppy in me whines
But this is fun or so I'm told.

Sorry folks, but I must go,
This party was fun, but I've hit a cog.
I think there's work for me at home.
I have to see a man about a dog.

We have talked but my battery is low,
My joy tires and the party mood sours.
There's a man and a dog, and I must go,
I'm afraid they've been waiting for hours.

Secrets

High tide comes slow and leaves quiet
Slinking away in the night like
It hid what it had to hide
And was done
The dock is silent
But for the lapping at the wood
And the breeze that strolls its way to sea
Keeping all the secrets
That came in on the last tide
They whisper between each other

And I know I'm eavesdropping
But they don't know and I don't care
I can't speak their language anyways
These words make as little sense to me
As the language spoken by the dawn
Only this language is
Lower and deeper and softer and quieter,
A language made for secret keeping
And for slinking away
Silent

In the night

Dear Pacific

If I reach just a little farther
I am sure I can reach those stars
Watch them scatter across my fingers
Like they are rings or they are scars
They could leave their trails of ivory light
To wind across my blemished skin
As I release them to the wild again
To go back to where they've already been
To leave me here with just the trail
They left for my hands to wash in the sea
So I could scatter that trail of forlorn light
Across a world that may let it run free

Birdsong

You that sings just ahead of the dawn
With your voice made of sand:
I hear you,
I understand.

And your porcelain voice paints the landscape
alive
When the night rests and the endless sky glows.
The wide marsh is thriving.
The honey flows.

You that brings this world home when you sing,
You are small and you are everything.

You that sings, I hear your voice.
I know what you mean when you wonder on low
Of things you and I could not possibly know.

The travellers hear you, but listen in passing.
They do not wait for you to say your message,
They care less for your words,

Take you for your visage.

You that sings for a world we don't have
anymore,
I watch the fires and I fear your song will end.
I don't know if you will survive it all again.

I hear your song, you wonder whether it's sunset
or smoke.
I wonder, too, for all these futures we've
planned.
I hear you.
I understand.

Meeting Dusk

It is known only as now and then and will be
Someday and Once Was and
It returns

The greatest known ever known
And a forward that cannot be seen
All happening at once

Because the sun is getting low and the sky erupts
And the stars are looking forward
The future of the past
They have seen it all

And the silence is impermeable
And the darkness is deafening
And the world moves towards wherever it's
going
The future and the someday and the past and the
once was
And all the right now that can fit around it
All at once where the sky ends

And turns dark